Rescue Workers

by Sunita Apte

⒞Harcourt
SCHOOL PUBLISHERS

Printed in the United States of America

ISBN 10: 0-15-351691-7
ISBN 13: 978-0-15-351691-7

Ordering Options
ISBN 10: 0-15-351216-4 (Grade 6 Advanced Collection)
ISBN 13: 978-0-15-351216-2 (Grade 6 Advanced Collection)
ISBN 10: 0-15-358174-3 (package of 5)
ISBN 13: 978-0-15-358174-8 (package of 5)

2 3 4 5 6 7 8 9 10   179   12 11 10 09 08 07

A man is trapped in an overturned car. A woman sits on her roof as floodwaters swirl around her. A couple is stuck under their overturned boat in raging seas. A family is frantically trying to escape from a burning building. All of these people need to be rescued. Who will help them?

Rescue workers will. They are the men and women who risk their lives every day to save others. They undergo difficult training and work long hours to be able to help people.

People left stranded after natural disasters, such as earthquakes and hurricanes, rely on rescue workers to save them. They know that these dedicated men and women won't stop until the last survivor is pulled from the rubble of an earthquake-destroyed building, or until the last people stranded by hurricane floods are plucked from the roofs of their houses.

Let's take a look at two different kinds of rescue workers. Rescue swimmers work in the water. They rescue those unfortunate enough to be stranded on or near oceans, lakes, and rivers.

Firefighters, on the other hand, work on land. They rescue people from burning buildings, cars, chemical explosions, and other disastrous situations.

Both types of rescue workers do highly specialized jobs. Both require enormous amounts of training and great bravery. Without them both, people would be a lot less safe.

Rescue Swimmers

A fishing boat is stranded off the Alaskan coast. A huge snowstorm has broken out over the ocean. Giant waves bombard the boat, tossing it around like a toy. It's only a matter of time before the boat sinks. Onboard are a man and his six-year-old son. They are far from shore and will not last long in the frigid water.

Fortunately, they have radioed a distress signal to the Coast Guard. Now a Coast Guard helicopter is on its way to help. Besides the pilot, there will be one other person onboard: a Coast Guard rescue swimmer. It will be the rescue swimmer's job to get the man and his son off the boat and to a safe, dry place.

The helicopter hovers at a low altitude over the boat. The plan is for the pilot to lower a rescue basket onto the boat, but the boat is being tossed about too much. The pilot can't get the rescue basket onto the boat. Instead, it lands in the water nearby.

Now the only chance for survival is for the man and boy to jump into the water and try to swim to the basket. If they make it, they will be saved. If they don't, they will almost certainly drown or die of exposure to the freezing water.

The father straps his son to his chest and jumps into the water. However, he has trouble getting to the rescue basket. In the meantime, the rescue swimmer onboard the helicopter has lowered himself into the turbulent ocean with a cable. He struggles to get the man and his son into the basket. After several suspenseful minutes, he succeeds. The man and his son are hoisted up to the hovering helicopter.

The rescue swimmer, however, is not so lucky. A giant sea swell catches him and drags him down. Fighting back to the surface, the rescue swimmer loses his mask and snorkel and injures his back.

He fights to stay afloat in the raging water until the rescue basket is lowered for him, and he climbs safely aboard. With the rescue completed, the helicopter heads back to the Alaskan coast. There, the man, his son, and the rescue swimmer will all get medical attention. Everyone onboard the helicopter, however, knows who is the real hero of the day. Without the rescue swimmer, the man and his son would have surely drowned in the icy Alaskan water. The swimmer risked his life and was injured, but he managed to do his job. He saved two lives.

The Coast Guard, the Navy, and the Air Force all have rescue swimmers. It takes a special kind of person to become one. Rescue swimmers must be willing to head into the water in all sorts of extreme conditions. They must be prepared to rescue people stranded on coastlines, on boats, and in the water. They need to know how to provide basic life support, which means they have to learn emergency medical training.

Becoming a rescue swimmer isn't easy. Over half the people who enter the training programs drop out. They aren't equipped for the grueling physical and mental endurance required of the job. Rescue swimmers have to stay calm in situations that cause most people to panic. To ensure they learn how to stay calm, their instructors are very hard on them. The rescue swimmer training course isn't for the fainthearted.

Even after passing the course, it isn't all smooth sailing. Rescue swimmers have to make sure that they stay in shape. They have to pass a required monthly physical training test that includes push-ups, pull-ups, sit-ups, chin-ups, a twelve-minute swim, an underwater swim, and towing another person through the water.

None of that is easy. However, it all counts when a rescue swimmer is out in the open water, fighting waves and pulling a victim to safety. Rescue swimmers have had to dangle off vertical cliffs to rescue stranded coastal hikers. They have had to battle surging tides along California's coast to rescue kids stuck in sea caves. Whatever the situation calls for, the rescue swimmer needs to be ready.

Fortunately, they have been. Since rescue swimmer programs were first started over forty years ago, thousands of lives have been saved by these brave men and women.

Firefighters

July 14, 2005: A disaster is about to overshadow this hot summer morning. People are waiting at a bus stop in New York City. Suddenly, a loud boom echoes down the block. Before people at the bus stop know what has happened, a shower of wood, concrete and metal comes crashing down on them.

A building has collapsed, pinning people in the rubble. Panic sets in on the block. A woman shouts, "My baby!" Five people, including a small baby, have been trapped in the debris of the fallen building. A stroller is just barely visible through a crack in the rubble.

Passersby try to dig people out. Soon, however, special rescue teams from the New York Fire Department arrive on the scene and take charge. They have been trained for this kind of situation. They know what to do in an emergency like this.

The rescue teams also know that if they don't get the baby and the others out soon, the victims' chances of survival begin to fade. Quickly, the rescue workers begin to claw at the debris with crowbars. They use saws to cut away steel and wood.

The minutes tick by as onlookers wait and watch. Will they get the people out in time? Is anyone severely injured? Fifteen minutes later, all five people, including the baby, have been freed. They are quickly rushed to local hospitals, along with five workers who were hurt during the rescue operation.

Five rescue workers were hurt trying to save five people. However, no lives were lost. That makes this rescue a success. Rescue workers hope that all their calls will turn out like this one.

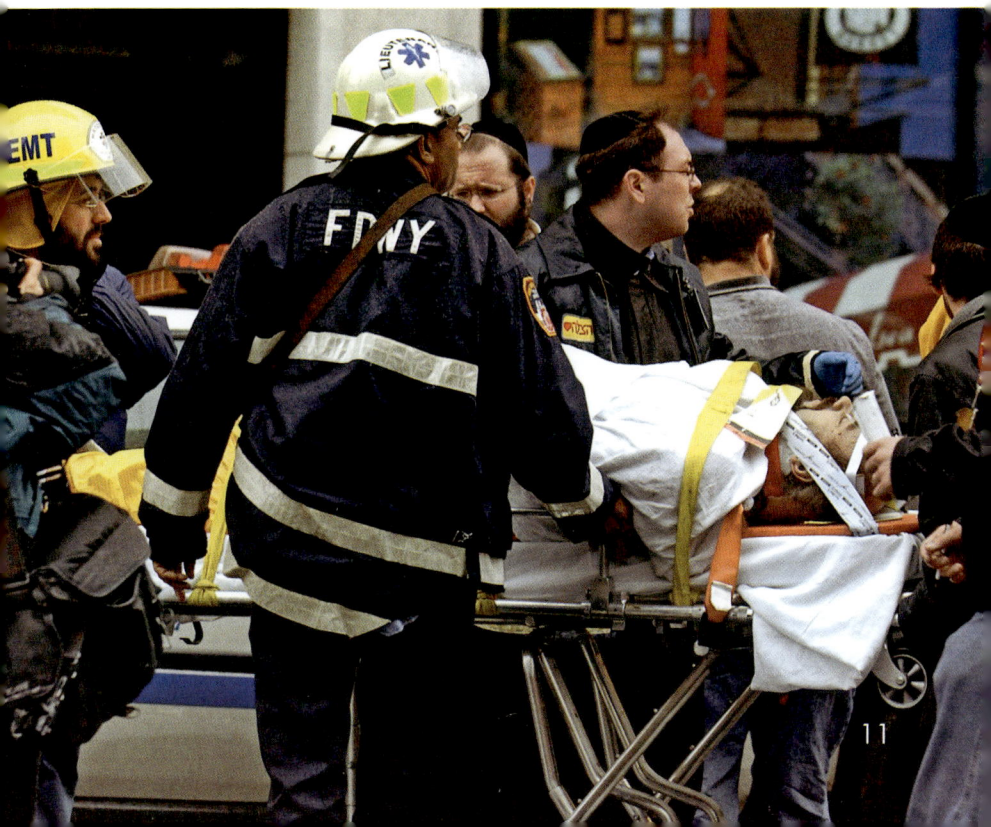

To some extent, all firefighters perform rescues. For one thing, they have to rescue people trapped in burning buildings. Large cities and towns, however, have special rescue squads. These squads are part of the fire department, but their members get special training that regular firefighters do not.

Rescue squad firefighters are trained to deal with collapsed buildings and hazardous waste. They know how to use special lifesaving equipment that can extricate people from crushed cars. Many of them also have emergency medical training. This makes them important first responders in any large disaster.

Rescue squads take charge of the most difficult fire rescues. However, they also respond to emergencies that are not fire-related. They respond to collapsed buildings and chemical spills. They show up when people are hit by a train or if a bridge falls down. In short, if something is on fire or people are in trouble, a rescue squad will almost certainly be one of the first squads to arrive.

The first rescue squad in the United States was established in New York in 1915. Soon after, other cities, such as Boston, followed suit. Even in those days, the early rescue squads did much more than fight fires. The rescue squad in Boston, for instance, responded to 294 alarms in its first ten months alone! Most of those calls were for fires. However, they also responded to calls about ammonia leaks, gas leaks, an elevator accident, and even a drowning.

Today's rescue squads are kept busy as well. In a big city, any given week might bring fires, a collapsed building, bad car wrecks, and a gas-line explosion. No one can predict what the next disaster might be, so rescue squads must be prepared for anything. They must be mentally prepared, which means keeping up on the latest rescue techniques and learning about how to deal with any hazard. They must also be physically prepared. Rescuing people often involves hard physical labor. Like rescue swimmers, rescue squad firefighters have to be in great shape. Unlike rescue swimmers, they don't have to be incredibly strong in the water. However, they definitely benefit from the same push-ups, sit-ups, pull-ups, and chin-ups that rescue swimmers do.

What's in store for rescue workers of the future? Well, they may be getting a little help. Many places are testing search and rescue robots. These robots may be better able to find their way through burning, smoky buildings. Unlike people, these reserve robotic rescuers will not be hampered by poisonous fumes or extremely high temperatures.

Search and rescue robots may also be able to fit through small holes in the rubble of collapsed buildings. Searching inside the rubble, robots could quickly discover the location of any survivors.

For now, though, rescue workers continue to be the first line of response in a disaster. That's why they must be well-trained and dedicated to their jobs. Rescue workers do dangerous work, but they know that it is important work. For many, saving lives is the best job they can imagine.

Think Critically

1. Why is it important that rescue workers be well trained both physically and mentally?

2. What is the main idea of this book? List three details that support the main idea.

3. What are two differences between a rescue swimmer's and a firefighter's job?

4. How does the author feel about rescue workers? How can you tell?

5. Would you rather be a rescue swimmer or a firefighter? Why?

Science

Make a Rescue Chart Create an illustrated chart showing different natural disasters and the kinds of rescue teams that would be required to respond to them.

School-Home Connection Discuss safety and rescue at home with family members. Create a family plan of action for what to do in case of a natural disaster.

Word Count: 1,722